Kósmos Sýnthesi

Matthew Barry

BookLeaf Publishing

India | USA | UK

Presentation by *BookLeaf Publishing*

Web: www.bookleafpub.com

E-mail: info@bookleafpub.com

ISBN: 9789358316858

First edition 2023

*To Kieran McGuigan, a shamefully
un-acknowledged poet.*

ACKNOWLEDGEMENT

To the great poets, whose names I can't recall.
Primarily Ezra Pound.

PREFACE

"A symphony must be like the world." so said the composer Gustav Mahler and this book strives to emulate the statement. I think the world is troubled at the minute and I think it is troubled in various ways that we refuse to acknowledge.

We tell ourselves lies as our lives are still comfortable, we just let someone else do it or we trust that professional people are as professional as they say. It leads us down a path of apathy and isolation, in my view, and it primarily prevents actions that would improve not just our lives but our fellow mortals' lives. It is merely that sense that I wish to capture in this book and that perhaps there would be catharsis that would bring about thought and perhaps principled action; like that of Antigone over Polynices.

Kósmos Sýnthesi

Colossi of Rhodes, a baton it holds,
Directs an orchestra across the world.
Up-raise the harp-sea;
The blackened chords of glee,
The clang and strike; the sonorous bell tolls.

And sonorous they sing as Cilician sons.
Farewell the doom on salt-sea sails;
The crescent of the sands,
The western music strands,
Discord that parts them, comes crush the chorus.

To the base of the Gaels, the trombones wail.
Sets of brass in the cloth-strewn pit astound,
Minds that came hereafter,
More musical masters,
Harpsichords in Greek ancestral dales.

It's there the symphony stalls,
About Ceuta, mouth of the worlds.
No man of Sophocles crossed the Doldrums,
Nor rhythmic beats of the galley fleets;
Feasting on the Maestro's rich-tea crumbs.
Except to the legends of the mermaid realms,
The vast untouched, nature's viola strings.

Lines of the world for the cradle's music sheet.

And thus the orchestra plays,
On it plays;
So it plays on,
And on it plays,
To the close of the days,
While musicians sway
To the moulding clay.

The Sombre Yard

The little hearts of the sombre yard,
Feet on the pavement clatter,
A pit-patter
On the latter
Past those long-gone
And old oaken fronds.

Running in the daytime to the safety of sun;
Holy water, garlic and blessed crucifix,
They that banished spirits
But young hearts bring the spring onion fix;
They couldn't actually buy it.
Slow walking at night underneath the
shadow-spun,
Seeing the man squatting by candles;
Moon's reflection of a half-man trundles
By the cremation avenue,
Dark-delve reaper in their view.

Still air greets them in the children's graveyard,
Hounded out by the phantasmal guard.
Under the lamppost light, safely and gay,
With stories to tell of adventurous day,
But the merry graves; they have naught to say.

Purple Portrait

She asked us timidly, with hair of auburn,
Or was it red? Or black? Or a shade of
blue-gold?
As the prismatic hair of Circe on her isle.
My memory decides on a purple byzantine.

A septum's bullring,
Pale skin of banshees,
Long locks like a wire brush;
To magnify strokes of mascara.

Oh I'm a man with will undone,
Her eyes seized the vampiric;
And I returned medusic,
Under the iron roses in the eves.
About her canvas, hands hid in sleeves,
And she asked us timidly: when will you come?
But the frame is cracked; the fissures and
ravines
And she's surrounded by more ravishing scenes.

Alarm at Five in the Morning

5

When I come home, there's no-one to be found,
Early-rise and late home; so's me round.
Pay in me savings and the bills on time,
Keeping a stern eye on village crime;
Everyman one of 'em knows me
It's a heartening respect to see.
So, when I sit down with my milky tea,
Remember them in my armchair tweed,
I snap-glance to my rear,
Listen with trained old ears,
The open door to the hallway:
In a house with not much to say.
Like someone should be standing there,
Well once, perhaps, someone was there;
And now, perhaps, there's no-one there
But the thought of that; it's too much to bear.

Aethyrialas, Angel of Miasma

With immaculate form stands
An angel, arms outstretched
Smiling wide, a caring gaze
To soothe our sudden ills;
A nausea born of a deeper malady.
A pink descending mist; sweet odour
To the sated nose. Burning through.
With blinking eyes,
We enter her miasma.

The angel stands unmoving.
Her image stagnating,
Mould festers at the smiles edge,
Eyes glazed over that meet the ground.
Light of the halo casts off shadows
That hide the slither of maggots
Boring tunnels through pure skin.
Fingertips darkened;
Feet encased in grime.
Its wings are wax to keep the fraying in
And unrelenting, we embrace
And desperately;
We feel the calming slither.

Ginger Fresco

The rim of the cup; see the steam rise up,
In the house of ideas, first to be,
Rather neglected in these years to see.
And I write in a style: The Forlorn Hope.

She, fire-touched, hair knotted in workers buns;
A figure sleek in her slave uniform,
One-by-one and sheltered from sun,
Dips and curves hidden by morn,
Eyes drawn to naturally stare;
While pretending she's not really there.

But she grabbed at my hand; made demand:
Come sit and talk; interrupt my work,
Why she's bored at her shift, just make it swift,
It's my suspicion inherent, a fair deterrent;
To a tear in the heart
But she kept up the start,
So true it's the captured smile,
That keeps me a longer while.

My work on the fresco stalled,
I think of braids twin-twining the crest,
Of deep set brown for Gaia's strength.
Just staring at me, the deep pits widen,

The thought of her ne'er to rest.
Barely lucid, my pen is hers,
The smile comes pierce the curse,
Firey desire longs to hear;
But through my own wretched fear,
She'll not hear this candid verse.

Filikó Axiothéato

In the Odeon Athenai, realm of crusade;
Strewn the tales in trails of red velvet.
Where the side-long glance,
And the mirrored stance,
Denote attraction in dulcet
Tones while sunset
Gleams the day we danced.

Such Persian lies,
In the personaii,
Of how the way supposedly goes,
Mere proximity supposedly shows;
Convey in masks of rage,
The swirling, twirling Nostrum stage,

Knowing what you've heard:
Mimic the sainted words,
Wearing the mask of glass.
Ah, but they can see you lurk in the grass
A deep stab at your heart's doing,
From your plucked oak's ruins
Set your own axe on the boughs hewing.

Laimergía

In deep of the mind, the little voice draws.
Littler than that one which drives our course,
No teeny tingling, a grey shade capturing
Will; it free-falls failing to resist suggesting.

Portioned out food to save from poverty,
Just two more; now two left, just finish fast;
But a bit sad; just can't cope; have a drink.
Older people drink more daily; just think:
Fatter than you have lost more weight in past,
The voice mimics the best with subtlety,
Portrays as good the sin of gluttony.

Lagneía

Buttery legs twine round locking closer
In the grape vine wound pressing up her
Loose skirts, while down goes her wool-dress
seams,
A flash of pleasure for damaged esteem.

It holds court in the keep of Hades' lowest crust,
For willing souls seeking momentary release.
No pain, and yet, the bruised and lonely seek;
Not reduction to an object to use thus:
Selfish degradation of others is worthy of their
lust.

Aplistía

Merchants only wish the contracts fair due.
No use gazing at me to resent,
Was your own will that gave consent,
Better that nihilism rings true;
Name them and say they lead miserable lives,
That they have no friends and loveless wives:
As bothersome to them as rain to a mole,
Or they'd have filled the needy bowls.

As those in power take more than they need,
The clink of gold excites them so,
Anger at them just merely grows,
The underserved weak forced to concede;
Under the wrenching squeeze of the sin called
greed.

Nothrótita

13

Why the lady outside the chemist's said:
"Its feeling numb but pleasurably spun
To sleep til' sleep is boring and done."
Prefers viewing weeds twining her bed,
Or so that's what she said.

She works her snout feeding from the credit
trough,
So free of laze, to work for pay, her time her
own,
So see her gaze, Time's long lost way, and
naught to show:
Another hour to while away the chewing moths,
But once, she had detested the sin of sloth.

Thymós

Weakness ever averse to rage,
But that's how the impotent build the cage.
Never to drive skewer through the hay,
Imagined slight that starts the fray;
Mere bellows on the Odeon stage.

For their own catharsis they choose this path,
To engage in rage cuts off the future sight,
No petitence enough for ill-thought fights;
More enemies made at the expense of a laugh
For future hard-bites for the sin of wrath.

Zilévo

Each day he lingers the house manor,
The gardens too verdant, the ceiling too tall;
They should be equal to this side of the wall,
He bet the owner had never held a hammer.

With a gang they ripped up the roses,
Culled the cakes and graffiti'd the gates,
The police never came; too busy they claimed,
Though the grounds are historic and famed.

A gran had lived there all her life,
Her father earned from the fish in fife,
From lowly boy then rich respectfully,
Now she's alone with no fit company,
Reduced to little by the sin of envy.

Yperifáneia

In splendid robe, the voice of the greats of
history,
With confidence they answer the deepest
mysteries.
Beckon us closer to encompassing light,
All our qualms banished from sight.

Wrapping worries with their linen cloths,
Evils excused by our thinning thirst:
Blot out the blood, the whole sea first,
To entrust our morals to greater minds.

But confidence is the hardest to hide,
There is now so little self-reflection,
They are right: no room for deflection;
And so are built the iron sides,
No compromise can even be tried.
You should know it's the deadliest sin,
For arrogance festers within,
Grinning atop the judge's throne;
Sits, leering, the horror of Pride.

Marble King

Oi pýles échoun pései kai zo akóma

Efficiency ruined and diplomacy garbled,
And the Army tired from corrupt dealings;
For the final stand they fight unyielding,
And he had thrown off his mantle,
To adopt the common soldiers sandal.
He'll be remembered, reborn, encased in
Marble.

On the Coast of Epirus

Ómorfi théa apó tin koryfí enós eléfanta
I Ípeiros etoimázetai na ekdikitheí ekeína ta lofía
kapnoú
Trapped at Justicia's beck and call,
For noble goals we'll gladly fall;
But even fighting for justice and right,
Can mean demise when lacking might.
The truth of it all should really be known,
As the mortal realm has cynically shown,
So often that life just isn't fair;
And the Epirote's march is doomed to despair.

The Greek Ireatos against the Latinitaium

Mr McGuigan, I say of you, foul Scotsman;
Your work of the verse it trips on the folly
Of high-heartedness, you lack melancholy,
On all that you sign, of way-back then.
How can you shoot the catharsis shot?
Of maidens and knights and all you've got?

Ask of Auden, Eliot and Pound,
Where's the misery our heroes expound.
So that's the play, the cut of your game,
Thy originality shall bleed into fame;
But the lack of recognition is such a shame.

How many poets could capture the verse,
In unforced ways without being terse.
Capture the natural talented miracle,
Of easy speech and waxing lyrical.

Ah, my friend, one day I suppose,
But you still yet live, much too verbose.

Black Samba

To the sway of the beat, the lum-drum thrum,
Comfort of a rocking seat, a well-placed bass,
Tap along under the guitar's harsh la-la,
Bang the head in the throng of her great long
song.

Lost in the locks of a spider maiden,
Under the stage n' the moshers ragin'
Caught her furtive in a side-long glance;
But in the roar of metal; there lacks the chance
And each of us goes our separate ways.
Silence with our friends in the darkling days,
Thus remains a landscape of dancing,
Amid the stomping, romping metal-mancing.
In that reverie they're always perfect,
Every memory becoming suspect.

Rhodian Slingers

Warm, roiling waves in the Rhodian days,
Pots and bronze swords on shop display.
Each man and woman, a wrinkling smiling face,
How the world so treats them is a damned
disgrace.

For their efforts to live so peacefully,
Their ways are mocked so scornfully;
Surrounded by foes whose hatreds simmer,
Those who understood just grow dimmer.

The ataturks are all in their graves,
And the diaposra's cannot be saved;
Those friends are shrinking them weaker,
Future of the waves are growing bleaker.

But what would I care under the bleaching sun,
Another bowl of olives for some;
They're serving us for a stoic's pay,
They'll never recapture the philosopher's days.

Victory Without Wings

Take flight thy beauties of vengeance;
Nubs of wings on porcelain shoulders,
Lurking in the rocks of the acropolis,
Talons reaching for the phantasmal Aegeus.
Aye, thy claws and deceitful beaks,
That work on sowing blood in the fields,
Attractive and dark or cold and sleek,
You've legs as sheenful as cream
And you furies have the dark-void eyes,
Oh aye, we fall for their hypnotise.

The priestesses at the temple summit,
Oh aye, their pure dresses hide their figure,
Hair is tended like olive trees.
White eyes as the sea foam of the Aegean,
They tend us well with their virtuous plight;
Under Athena and her justiciable sight,
But there she stands alone and virginal,
Cleanly sword and her shield vestigial.

Aye, we men, we're vengeance seekers,
Despite our comfort with those much weaker;
The draw's too strong of the furies bleaker.
Athena's justice rained,
Her wings were gained,

And Victory obtained,
With a rule of feathers enveloping,
The cavern furies orac'ling,
Oh aye, we go on stepping;
Into the dark, and danger knowing.

Their gazes work to turn us to thralls,
Shudder to think of gliding gulls;
So see, we love their corruption,
A deathly slight to her wingless eruption.

Blonde Tarantella

Always astride the raucous laughter
And swear the she's be more frequent than he's.
Overflowing with bubbly energy,
And an impression that left thereafter.

Oh, the back-step of spontaneity,
The rush forward of sincerity;
Side-long la of the ga-la-la,
Energy of a ra-cha-cha.

It's a dance on the lance of Calabria,
On dagger Stiletto's, the moves of Española;
Be drawn all closer by their energy,
And banished of bare entropy,
Enraptured by sun-shredded blondity,
Oh, the energetic oddities.

www.ingramcontent.com/pod-product-compliance
Lightning Source LLC
LaVergne TN
LVHW051247200726
843510LV00011B/1717